Pirates Coming T.

Hide your money,
your gold, and jewels, too.

Yo ho, yo ho!

Pirates coming through!

Pirates sail ships
to faraway lands
in search of great treasure
buried in sand.

4

Pirates are rowdy.

Pirates are mean.

Pirates don't whisper.

They yell, shout, and scream.

Shiver me timbers!
Hoist the main sail!
Pull up the anchor!
Hold on to the rail!

Hide your money,
your gold, and jewels, too.

Yo ho, yo ho!

Pirates coming through!

Speaking of manners,
pirates have none.
When there's food on the table,
they grab some and run.

Never a **"please"**
or a **"thank you"** you'll hear.
Just rude talk and squabbles
when pirates are near.

But at the end of a swashbuckling day,
even pirates get tired and say,

"Good night me mateys.

Good night, good night.

Anyone have time for one little . . .

fight!"

Hide your money,
your gold, and jewels, too.

Yo ho, yo ho!

Pirates coming through!